BIGGEST NAMES IN MUSIC

BRUNO MARS

by Martha London

T0014713

FOCUS
READERS

NAVIGATOR

WWW.FOCUSREADERS.COM

Focus Readers is distributed by North Star Editions:
sales@northstareditions.com | 888-417-0195

Produced for Focus Readers by Red Line Editorial.

Photographs ©: Matt Sayles/Invision/AP Images, cover, 1, 4–5, 7; Kevin Mazur/WireImage/MTV/Getty Images, 8–9; Scott Boehm/AP Images, 11, 18; Catherine McGann/Hulton Archive/Getty Images, 13; Chris Pizzello/AP Images, 14–15; Shutterstock Images, 17, 29; PG/Splash News/Newscom, 20–21; Evan Agostini/AP Images, 22; Charles Sykes/Invision/AP Images, 25; John Angelillo/UPI/Newscom, 27

Library of Congress Cataloging-in-Publication Data
Names: London, Martha, author.
Title: Bruno Mars / by Martha London.
Description: Lake Elmo, MN : Focus Readers, 2021. | Series: Biggest names in music | Includes index. | Audience: Grades 4-6
Identifiers: LCCN 2020013667 (print) | LCCN 2020013668 (ebook) | ISBN 9781644936368 (hardcover) | ISBN 9781644936450 (paperback) | ISBN 9781644936634 (pdf) | ISBN 9781644936542 (ebook)
Subjects: LCSH: Mars, Bruno, 1985---Juvenile literature. | Singers--United States--Biography--Juvenile literature. | Musicians--United States--Biography--Juvenile literature.
Classification: LCC ML3930.M318 L66 2021 (print) | LCC ML3930.M318 (ebook) | DDC 782.42164092 [B]--dc23
LC record available at https://lccn.loc.gov/2020013667
LC ebook record available at https://lccn.loc.gov/2020013668

Printed in the United States of America
Mankato, MN
082020

ABOUT THE AUTHOR

Martha London writes books for young readers full-time. She enjoys all types of music. In high school and college, she spent several years performing in musicals.

TABLE OF CONTENTS

CHAPTER 1

AT THE GRAMMYS

Singers lined the stage at the 60th Grammy Awards. A live band played next to them. They were performing the hit song "Finesse." The drummer pounded a quick beat. Then Cardi B took the stage. She and Bruno Mars had recorded "Finesse" together. Now they were performing it at the Grammys.

Bruno Mars moves to the music during his performance at the 60th Grammy Awards.

Cardi B rapped to start the song. Then Mars began to sing. He and his backup singers danced. Blocks of red, green, and yellow light flashed behind them.

After the first verse, Mars stepped back from his microphone and danced. The backup singers sang the chorus. Then Mars sang as he walked down a set of stairs to another small stage. There, he tossed his microphone aside and danced some more. The crowd clapped and cheered as he showed off his amazing moves.

After the dance break, Cardi B returned to the stage. She rapped as Mars sang. Their lively performance had the whole

Cardi B and Mars wore bright-colored clothes based on fashion from the 1990s.

room dancing. When the song ended, the audience burst into applause.

That evening, Mars received seven Grammy Awards. Mars was thrilled. His whole life, he'd wanted nothing more than to sing and perform. And that dream was coming true.

CHAPTER 2

BORN TO PERFORM

Peter Gene Hernandez was born on October 8, 1985, in Honolulu, Hawaii. When he was a toddler, his father gave him the nickname "Bruno." That became the name everyone called him.

Bruno grew up in a big family. He has five siblings. His family did not have a lot of money. They lived in a small house.

Bruno and his father, Pete Hernandez, attend the MTV Video Music Awards together in 2013.

For a while, this house didn't have a bathroom. But Bruno had a good childhood. He and his family were close.

One of the things Bruno loved about his childhood was the music. There was always music playing at home. His father played **percussion**. His mother was a singer and dancer. Instruments were always available. Bruno taught himself how to play drums, piano, and guitar.

In the evenings, Bruno and his family went to the variety show his dad and uncle put on. In this show, singers performed songs from the 1950s and 1960s. Bruno began performing in the show when he was four years old.

Bruno sometimes plays drums at his concerts. This bass drum has his mother's name, Bernadette, on it.

Music made Bruno happy. But he was bullied in school. Kids made fun of him for his **heritage**. Bruno's mother was Filipino. His father is Jewish and Puerto Rican.

Bruno tried not to let the bullying get to him. In high school, he formed a band with some of his friends. They called themselves the School Boys.

Bruno hoped to be a musician when he grew up. When he graduated from high school, he decided to leave Hawaii.

THE YOUNGEST ELVIS

Elvis Presley was one of the most popular singers of the 1950s and 1960s. Bruno sang songs by Elvis in his family's variety show. Bruno performed as an Elvis impersonator. He dressed up like Elvis. He tried to sing and act like him, too. As Bruno got older, he wanted to keep performing. But he wanted to make his own music.

Four-year-old Bruno prepares to perform as an Elvis impersonator in August 1990.

He moved to Los Angeles, California. To have a career in music, he felt he needed to be where the **producers** were.

CHAPTER 3

A START AS A SONGWRITER

In Los Angeles, Mars struggled to make enough money to pay his bills. He sang for several people who worked at record **labels**. He hoped they would offer him a **contract**. But most didn't think he was ready to be a professional singer.

Mars thought record labels might be more interested if he wrote his own music.

Mars often writes songs that are inspired by musical styles from the past.

A friend helped him write songs and bring them to producers. The producers liked the songs. But they didn't want Mars to sing them. They suggested having other artists perform the songs instead.

Mars decided to put his performing career to the side. He focused on writing songs for other artists. Mars formed a team with two friends. They wrote several hit songs in the early 2000s. Musicians and producers were eager to work with them. Mars still wasn't performing. But he didn't give up his dream.

In 2010, he got a chance to show his skills. Mars wrote a song for a rapper named B.o.B. Mars sang in the recording.

Mars wrote and produced songs as part of a team called the Smeezingtons.

When the song came out, **critics** praised Mars's voice. Producers finally asked him to make an album.

Mars released *Doo-Wops & Hooligans* in October 2010. It included "Grenade" and "Just the Way You Are." Both songs reached No. 1 on *Billboard*'s Hot 100.

More than 115 million viewers watched Mars perform in the halftime show for Super Bowl XLVIII.

Mars was on his way to becoming a star. He began his first **headlining** tour later that year.

Mars released his second album in December 2012. *Unorthodox Jukebox* received mixed reviews from critics. But the singles "Locked Out of Heaven" and

"Treasure" were hits on the radio. And the album eventually won a Grammy Award.

Mars planned a world tour to promote his new album. Then tragedy struck. His mother died suddenly. Mars was stunned. But he kept performing. He even did the halftime show at the Super Bowl in 2014.

AT THE SUPER BOWL

Performing the Super Bowl halftime show is a big honor. The show has featured famous musicians such as Madonna, Prince, and the Rolling Stones. Mars's performance in 2014 got many positive reviews. He was part of a second halftime show in 2016. That time, he performed alongside Beyoncé and Coldplay.

CHAPTER 4

FINDING THE MAGIC

Mars was eager to record more music. But he wasn't sure what he wanted his next album to sound like. Then Mark Ronson contacted him. Ronson is a singer and songwriter. He had helped Mars with *Unorthodox Jukebox*. Ronson asked Mars to **collaborate** on a song.

Mars and Mark Ronson (right) accept an MTV Video Music Award for "Uptown Funk."

In addition to singing, Mars plays a variety of instruments.

Ronson and Mars wrote "Uptown Funk" together. They released it in November 2014. The upbeat dance tune was an instant hit on the radio. It spent 14 weeks at the top of *Billboard*'s Hot 100. That set a new record for the longest-running song at No. 1.

After this success, Mars began working on his third album. But he continued having trouble. So, he tried rewriting the songs to get the sound he wanted. A few went through more than a dozen versions.

FINDING THE RIGHT SOUND

Mars spent long days in the studio when he was recording his third album. Sometimes he stayed there until three o'clock in the morning. And when he finally left, he brought a CD with the album's songs on it. Mars listened to this CD in the car. Sometimes he kept playing the songs in his driveway at home to work on them even more.

Eventually, all of his hard work paid off. Mars released *24K Magic* in November 2016. The album featured an electric piano and tinny cymbals. Those sounds were popular during the 1990s. Mars hoped to remind listeners of a time when they were young and happy.

Fans loved the new album. It sold nearly 230,000 copies in its first week. And within nine months, it sold more than one million copies. Critics liked the new music, too. Mars received seven Grammy **nominations** in 2017. He won all seven awards. They included Record of the Year and Song of the Year. When accepting the awards, Mars said he just wanted to make

Mars shows off his awards at the 60th Grammy Awards.

an album people could dance to. He was thrilled that so many people loved it.

Mars did not grow up with a lot of money. Now that he is wealthy, he wants to use his success to help people in need.

He often donates money to help others. For example, Typhoon Yolanda hit the Philippines in 2014. The strong storm destroyed many homes. People did not have a place to live. Mars gave $100,000 to help children affected by the storm.

In 2017, Mars gave $1 million to people in Flint, Michigan. Studies had shown that the water in Flint was not safe to drink. Residents had to use bottled water to drink and cook with. Mars donated money to help fix the water treatment plants. But as of 2020, Flint still didn't have clean water.

Whether giving money to important causes or making music that brings

The Revlon Concert for the Rainforest Fund helped support the rights of indigenous communities.

people joy, Mars tries to make the world a better place. Fans love his fun music and dance moves. They are eager to see what he does next.

BRUNO MARS

- Birth date: October 8, 1985
- Birthplace: Honolulu, Hawaii
- Family members: Pete (father), Bernadette (mother, deceased), Jaime (sister), Eric (brother), Tiara (sister), Presley (brother), Tahiti (sister)
- High school: Roosevelt High School
- Major accomplishments:
  - January 2014: *Unorthodox Jukebox* wins Best Pop Vocal Album at the Grammy Awards.
  - February 2014: Mars performs in the halftime show for Super Bowl XLVIII.
  - November 2014: Mars and Mark Ronson release the hit song "Uptown Funk."
  - January 2018: Mars wins seven Grammys for his album *24K Magic*.

Mars plays guitar during a concert in Milan, Italy, in 2011.

- Quote: "For me there's a process that I have to go through with each song. I have to touch an instrument or it won't come out. If I'm not touching the guitar or touching the drum machine or playing the piano, the song just won't come out. I have to be in it, all the way."

Hamish MacBain. "Bruno Mars: The Full NME Cover Interview." *New Musical Express*. NME, 18 Nov. 2016. Web. 5 Mar. 2020.

FOCUS ON
BRUNO MARS

Write your answers on a separate piece of paper.

1. Write a paragraph summarizing the main ideas of Chapter 3.

2. Do you think it is important for pop stars to use their fame to help others? Why or why not?

3. How old was Mars when he began performing in his family's variety show?
    - **A.** four years old
    - **B.** six years old
    - **C.** nine years old

4. How might going on a tour help an artist promote a new album?
    - **A.** A tour can keep the album from being reviewed by critics.
    - **B.** A tour can help more people hear and be excited about the new songs.
    - **C.** A tour is the only way for fans to hear the new songs.

Answer key on page 32.

GLOSSARY

collaborate
To work together on a project.

contract
An agreement that a musician makes to work with a specific recording company.

critics
People who review music and give their thoughts on it.

headlining
Performing as the main group or star of a concert.

heritage
Part of people's identity that comes from their community or family, especially when passed down over time.

labels
Companies that help artists put out music.

nominations
When people, songs, or albums are chosen as finalists for an award or honor.

percussion
Instruments played by being hit or shaken, such as drums or bells.

producers
People who work with musicians to record songs.

TO LEARN MORE

BOOKS

Lajiness, Katie. *Bruno Mars: Famous Musician*. Minneapolis: Abdo Publishing, 2018.

National Geographic Kids. *Turn It Up! A Pitch-Perfect History of Music That Rocked the World*. Washington, DC: National Geographic Kids, 2019.

Rajczak Nelson, Kristen. *Bruno Mars: Singer and Songwriter*. New York: Enslow Publishing, 2017.

NOTE TO EDUCATORS

Visit **www.focusreaders.com** to find lesson plans, activities, links, and other resources related to this title.

INDEX

Answer Key: 1. Answers will vary; **2.** Answers will vary; **3.** A; **4.** B